This book is a gift to:

Suki

From:

Mum & Bunny

Date:

Christmas 2008.

Precious time with Others

Strengthen your relationships

NINA SMIT

CHRISTIAN ART
PUBLISHERS

Originally published by Christian Publishing Company
under the title *Maak tyd vir ander*

© 1997
First edition 1999

CHRISTIAN ART
P O Box 1599, Vereeniging, 1930

Translated by Esta Grobler
Cover designed by Christian Publishing Company

Scripture taken from the HOLY BIBLE, NEW INTERNATIONAL
VERSION. Copyright © 1973, 1978, 1984 by International
Bible Society. Used by permission of Zondervan Publishing House.

Set in 11 in 13 pt Souvenir by Christian Publishing Company

Printed and bound in Singapore

ISBN 1-86852-420-5

© All rights reserved. No part of this book may be reproduced in any
form without permission in writing from the publisher, except in the
case of brief quotations embodied in critical articles or reviews.

99 00 01 02 03 04 05 06 07 08 – 10 9 8 7 6 5 4 3 2 1

Dedicated to:

Anneli, who always has time for others.

Foreword

As the years carry on we realise two things: time passes by quicker and we have less time on our hands! We do not even have enough time to do our own things, and it is almost inevitable that our relationships with others are neglected because of it ... Your own family is usually the first to suffer under your heavy workload and limited time, because they are the ones who do not complain! In due course you find that you do not have time for your friends, that you do not have the time to see people in need and to reach out to them.

Make time – time for your family, time for your friends, time for other people. Time to love the people closest to you; time to appreciate your friends; time to mean something to those who may need you. We cannot experience true happiness without other people. We need other people – therefore we have to learn to make time for others.

Invest in your marriage

The fact that two out of every three marriages in South Africa end in divorce, tells us that most people do not have the right attitude towards marriage. A successful marriage is not the result of everlasting love; it is rather an opportunity to love, a promise that has to be kept. A happy marriage demands hard work. "A successful marriage requires a divorce," says Paul Frost, "a divorce from your self love."

To make a success of your marriage requires the putting aside of your own interests. Making time for your partner. Time to talk. Time to often do things together. These things do not have to cost money ... Time to be there for each other, to listen to each other and to grow closer to God. The ultimate guarantee for a marriage that is truly happy is for both partners to serve and love the Lord.

Marriage is what the two of you go through together. The greater

Invest in your marriage

your appreciation of each other, the more fulfilling the marriage. (John Drescher)

Marriage is ... keeping watch at a sickbed together, struggling through the budget together, a thousand good night kisses and early morning smiles, holidays at the sea and conversations in the dark, a growing appreciation of each other that originates from mutual respect and love. (George Sweazy)

To love your husband is not a strong, intense feeling. It is an act of your will, it is an assessment of value, it is a promise. (Erich Fromm)

It's a good thing to take stock of the true meaning of your marriage, to examine what you are investing in your relationship, for yourself and the person next to you. Such an evaluation will open your eyes to what you and your spouse will be left with someday. (Alba Bouwer)

Make time for each other

- Talk a while before you go to sleep at night.
- Bring your wife coffee and rusks in bed.
- Buy his or her favourite magazine or sweets when you go to town.

Invest in your marriage

- Do not complain to your friends about each other.
- Remember that there is no marriage without quarrels.
- Wash his back in the bath.
- Fill a deep bubble bath for her.
- Take the same care of yourself as in the days of your engagement.
- Listen carefully to what your partner has to say.
- Take care to balance the budget.
- Share your thoughts, dreams, ideals and fears with each other.
- Remember to kiss each other goodbye when you part.
- Say and show that you love each other every day, and make sure that the children see it.
- Surprise your spouse with unexpected, spontaneous things that melt his/her heart.
- Do not expect each other to look the same as twenty years ago.
- Pretend not to see your husband's growing bald spot.
- Prepare his favourite meal.
- Enjoy coffee at your favourite coffee shop.
- Show interest in his work and invite his colleagues to dinner.
- Offer to make dinner if she looks tired.
- Encourage each other on your "down" days.
- Wash his car or ask one of the children to mow the lawn if he has a hectic work schedule.

Invest in your marriage

- Do not take the things she does at home for granted.
- Hold hands in church.
- Accompany him to a rugby game sometimes.
- Accompany her to an art gallery sometimes.
- Make a list of everything you appreciate in her and stick it on the inside of her closet door.
- Help her with the dishes or to tidy the kitchen.
- Give each other a sincere compliment every day.
- Immediately sew on his shirts' buttons that have come off.
- Repair the leaking kitchen tap before she asks you to.
- Surprise him with a new shirt, tie or pyjamas.
- Make a special day of your anniversary and Father's and Mother's Day.

Make time for each other's primary needs

$\mathcal{D}$r. William Harley, an American marriage counsellor, studied the preferences of men and women for twenty years. The findings of almost 15 000 questionnaires showed that men and women have totally different basic needs. According to Harley's questionnaire the greatest need of a married man is sexual fulfilment, and secondly a beautiful, sensual wife! On the other hand, the two most important things women want from their spouses are affection and communication.

If wives realised what a positive effect it would have on their marriages if they took the trouble to be sensual to their husbands, there would be fewer broken marriages. Accordingly, a husband can secure his marriage if he remembers the fact that affection and communication are more important to his wife than sex.

Make time for each other's primary needs

Make time to cherish your love

- Charm your husband – invest in a sensual satin night-gown or lace underwear.
- Buying flowers or perfume for your wife shouldn't be a luxury.
- Make hotdogs for the children and send them to bed early. Then treat your husband to a candle light dinner.
- Write a love poem especially for her and put it under her pillow.
- Be original in the bedroom.
- Buy a paper-bag with love letter-sweets and give her one every day after dinner.
- Read a chapter from Song of Songs together.
- Put a red rose on his desk.
- Design a special Valentine's card for her.
- Leave a loving message on his cell phone or answering machine.
- Buy a special mug with hearts on it and pour your husband's tea in it.
- Tell your spouse every day why you think he or she is wonderful.
- Read love poems in front of the fireplace.
- Sex ought to be fun. Laugh more in the bedroom, as well as in the rest of the house.

Make time for each other's primary needs

- Be mysterious so that your husband never knows exactly what you are thinking.
- Put away your shyness and tell your husband what you do and do not like.
- Sex is a skill that has to be acquired – take care not to remain a novice.
- Fondle your wife in front of the children.
- Be curious about your sexuality and remember: nothing venture, nothing gain!
- Be sensitive to your spouse's sexual desires and needs.
- Look your best each day.
- Surprise your wife with two movie tickets (for a romantic movie) or rent a video.
- Write a love letter to your husband and hide it under his pillow.
- Do not walk past each other without touching each other.
- Go on a date once a week. This doesn't have to cost money – only time!
- Try to spend a weekend away, without the children, once every three months.
- If your spouse suddenly invites you some place, do not think of excuses – go!
- Ensure that your honeymoon lasts forever.

Your children need you

One of the biggest mistakes parents make, is to give their children toys and money instead of love and time. You do not owe your children luxuries, but you do owe them unconditional love and enough time to ensure that you really communicate and share thoughts.

Children cannot be brought up without discipline, but parents have to guard against constantly criticising and scolding them. Praise and appreciation achieve much more in children than criticism and sarcasm. Assure each of your children *every day* of your love. Show them that they are important and precious to you, and that you trust them. Children that are brought up this way, will not disappoint their parents when they are grown-ups.

However, remember that you are a person in your own right and that your children will not stay with you forever. Do not allow them to take up *all* your time – do things just for yourself sometimes. And

Your children need you

make sure they understand that your spouse is your first priority.

Your children need your presence more than your presents. (Jesse Jackson)

Successful parenthood does not require knowledge or riches or prestige. It requires people with principles and wisdom to handle them; people with love and insight, people who live enthusiastically. (Johan Heyns)

Give your child a mirror rather than an album full of portraits of his ancestors, a Bible rather than a sturdy bank account. (A.M. Wells)

The modern father often complains that he doesn't have enough time to spend with his children. But maybe the amount of time is not as important as the image of himself that he leaves with his son or daughter. If you do not provide your children with understanding, compassion, safety and visible love, you may spend the whole day at home, and your presence will still mean nothing to them. (J.M. Braude)

Make time for your children

- Starting when they are little, tell your children why they were baptised. Let them grow up in the embrace of God's love.

Your children need you

- Live your faith, so that your children will see it in everything you do and say.
- Make time for family devotions and pray together.
- Do not overprotect your children – it robs them of essential self-confidence.
- Respect your children's privacy and *never* go through their drawers or read their diaries or personal letters.
- Take your children for a visit to the zoo.
- Allow your children to learn from their own mistakes.
- Write a good reference about each child and stick in on their bedroom doors.
- Faithfully attend your children's school meetings, prize-givings and sporting events.
- Do not tell your children one thing and then do something else.
- Bake pancake together when it rains!
- Undertake a family project: build a swimming pool, make a rose garden or save for a dream holiday.
- Give your children "exam sweets" when they are studying.
- Encourage your children to work for their pocket money.
- Give each of your children individual attention – invite one at a time for a milkshake or a movie.
- Do not expect your children to share your taste in music and clothes.

Your children need you

- Do not compare your children with each other – acknowledge each child's personal talents.
- Each child should have specific responsibilities at home that he has to see to. Do not let a day pass without giving each of your children a special hug.
- Pray for each of your children every day.
- Do not expect more from your child than he is able to give.
- Do not criticise your children unnecessarily, rather praise them for the things they achieve.
- Start taking your children to church with you when they are little.
- Listen to your children and do your best to answer their trick questions.
- Give your children the freedom to make their own decisions.
- You owe your children understanding, safety and love, but not the luxuries modern children are used to.
- Do not offer your child gifts and money instead of time and attention.
- Often play with your children, even if you are not really fond of "Monopoly" or "Pictionary."
- Be sure that time spent with your children is quality time.
- Tell your children that you love them and show them that you trust them.

Your children need you

- Start teaching them good manners when they are little.
- Build your child's self-esteem; tell him that you are proud of him.
- Laugh more with your children.
- Keep a journal of your family jokes.
- Attend your children's prize-givings and sporting events, even if they are very boring.
- Support your children during crises.
- Discuss your finances openly with your children so that they do not expect more from you than you can afford.
- Provide your teenagers with extra love and understanding.
- Do not hesitate to ask your children's forgiveness when you have treated them unfairly.
- Children do not know right from wrong by themselves – it is your job to spell it out to them.
- House rules are necessary – be sure that your children keep them and punish them if they break the rules.
- Make a feast day of your children's birthdays – with a special birthday cake.
- Children who grow up without discipline are usually bound for disaster. Discipline your children from the start.
- Teach your children the right values: kindness, honesty, unselfishness and firmness of principle.

 *Your children need you*

- Make mealtimes special family times and do not eat in front of the television.
- Be sure that every child has a Christmas stocking to hang next to the Christmas tree.
- Teach your children the true meaning of Christmas.
- Make sure that your children will one day remember their childhood with love and appreciation.

The value of friends

The older one gets, the more one becomes aware of the value of friendship. Phil Bosmans knows what it is all about when he writes, "Friends are to people what sunlight is to flowers." Without the right friends to support you in bad times and to share your joys, life would be colourless and boring.

But true friendship requires sacrifice, because you need to make time for your friends, and nowadays very few people have the time just to pay a casual visit. True friendship also demands openness between friends – and it is difficult, because that means exposing yourself to getting hurt at the same time. However, friendship is worth the trouble and time we make for it. A person with friends is a rich human being – therefore make time in your busy schedule for your friends. Time to talk, time to listen, to be quiet, to be together – because time with friends is quality time!

The value of friends

A person who can share his joys with a friend, doubles it; and he who can trust a friend with his pain, halves it. An hour spent with a friend gives more insight into one's problems than a whole day spent alone and worrying about it. (Francis Bacon)

A friend. The hand of someone who wants to walk with you, who wants to travel along the same road – you are not alone any more. Two friends do not look so much at each other, together they look ahead. They do not search for each other, together they search for the things each one needs. Friends do not monopolise each other, because that will ruin the friendship. (Phil Bosmans)

I have found the essence of life: friendship! People often treat it carelessly, but it is the only thing that counts and that makes life bearable. (Terence Rattigan)

I can be totally honest with my friend. I may think out loud in front of him. I may act spontaneously, I don't have to pretend to be anything I am not. (Ralph Waldo Emerson)

A true friend talks freely, advises fairly, supports readily, defends bravely and does not change. (William Penn)

Make time for your friends

◆ Never be too busy to visit your friends – make time for them.

The value of friends

- If you do not have time to pay a visit, phone to say that you are thinking of them.
- Never gossip about your friends – and remember, friends who gossip with you, will most probably also gossip *about* you.
- Do not force your personal opinions and tastes upon your friends – be willing to differ from them and still love them.
- Give them the free use of your holiday cottage.
- Contact friends you haven't seen since your youth.
- Pray faithfully for your friends.
- Do not make friends for your own personal benefit.
- Be willing to make the time to listen to your friends.
- Let them finish talking without interrupting them.
- Do not place conditions on your friendship.
- Keep the secrets your friends share with you.
- Offer to look after your friend's three children under five years for a whole day.
- Visit your friends when in hospital.
- Support your friends in crisis situations or when they are sad.
- Surprise your friends with an unexpected gift, visit or flowers.
- Buy your friend a surprise gift and wrap it with special care.
- Make time to really listen to your friend, and then also share your innermost thoughts with your friend.
- Offer to look after your friends' pets when they are on holiday.

The value of friends

- Invite your friends to a meal that doesn't involve much preparation.
- Be willing to share your problems with your friends – they will probably suggest solutions that will be of much help to you.
- Tell or write your friend a letter in which you say what you appreciate most in her.
- Make new friends – enter into a conversation with someone that looks like a soulmate and invite her to tea.
- Try to complain less to your friends.
- Bake a batch of rusks for a working friend.
- Invite your friend for cheesecake and coffee or a real tearjerker movie.
- Be available to your friends.
- Be willing to talk to your friends when they do the wrong thing.
- Always be hospitable to your friends.

Forgiveness is therapy

It isn't always easy to forgive people who hurt and offend you. It is almost impossible to meet Jesus' requirement of forgiveness by forgiving seventy times seven (see Matt. 18:21-22). However, people who live in the past and pry on that unhappiness are sick, discontented people. On the other hand, people who have learned to forgive others just as the Lord is willing to forgive us each time, are people whose hearts are filled with peace.

Martin Lloyd Jones writes, "The man who has truly received forgiveness, and who knows it, is the man who can forgive others." Every Christian should therefore be willing to forgive the people who have offended him – because is it not what God is willing to do for us each day? If we read our Bible, we cannot but be aware of the price God had to pay to be able to forgive us. Therefore we may not keep our forgiveness from others. Especially in our country, forgiveness should play a very important role. Every person who wants to be happy, should make the time to forgive and forget the crimes of the past.

> The ability to forgive and to love are the weapons God has given us to tackle life with zeal, courage and honour in a less-than-perfect world. (H.S. Kushner)
>
> After everything people have experienced and endured from each other, peace can only come through forgiveness! Every word and every gesture that offer forgiveness, are a contribution towards peace. Forgiveness is the disarmament of the heart. Forgiveness is the most beautiful gift. Forgiveness costs more than giving. Therefore, forgive! (Phil Bosmans)
>
> Forgiveness is a small miracle. Forgiveness is a new beginning. Forgiveness is to begin over and to start working on your relationship with the one that has hurt you. God invented forgiveness as the only way to preserve his love relationship with mankind. (Lewis B. Smedes)
>
> The man who refuses to forgive others, destroys the bridge he himself will have to cross someday. All people are in need of forgiveness. (Thomas Fuller)

Make time for reconciliation

- Always be willing to forgive the people who have hurt you.
- If you have something against someone, do not cherish your bitterness; go and talk to the person.
- Be willing to be the first to say, "I'm sorry."
- If someone is angry with you, find out how you can restore your relationship.
- Be willing to forgive more than once. Remember what Jesus told Peter – seventy times seven!
- Forgive unconditionally.
- Do your best not only to forgive the people who have offended you, but also to forget what they have done.
- Also forgive yourself when you fail, and do not worry about mistakes from the past.
- Put your forgiveness into words – write a letter to say that you have forgiven someone with your whole heart.
- If you are unable to forgive someone completely, confess your unforgiveness to God.
- Be willing to start over with someone who has hurt your trust.
- Ask God to help you to forgive a person if you can't do it by yourself.

Make time to help others

The way you think and act, determines the way other people will behave towards you. Look around you at the large circle of friends of a person who really cares. On the other hand, introverts who are unwilling to reach out to others, have very few friends. The Bible teaches us that we have to help and support others in crisis situations. We should make time to become involved in the problems of the people around us.

Unfortunately, thoughtful people are hard to find, but each one of us can learn to recognise people in crisis situations, to care for them and to reach out to them. If you have empathy with other people, you have to show it through your works. By caring and helping, you reveal your own gratitude for the things God gives you.

Therefore, make time to become aware of the needs of the people around you and to do something about it. Sometimes do kind

Make time to help others

things just to make life more enjoyable for others. By thinking and acting positively you can make a difference in the world you live in.

> When people feel the heart of a fellow human being, they come alive. Somewhere inside of you is an angel waiting with a message of goodness and love for the people on earth. Let him be seen in your actions. (Phil Bosmans)
>
> Love isn't only ingenious in the offering of help, it is in the first place ingenious in the awareness of need. It reveals the suffering of our fellowman to us. Before love sets our hands in motion, it opens our eyes. (Helmut Thielicke)
>
> The man who is a true neighbour to others, is willing to risk his position, prestige, even his life for the sake of others. In the dark valleys, along the dangerous heights of life's road he will see and help a defenceless and fainthearted brother. (Martin Luther King)

Make time to be thoughtful

- Always be the first to say hello.
- Give other drivers a gap in rush hour.
- Write a letter to your favourite teacher from your schooldays and tell him how he has influenced your life positively.

Make time to help others

- If you hear of a family that suffers financially, offer your help.
- Always be positive and friendly, but be sure that your friendliness is never artificial.
- Share your star recipe with a friend.
- Join the SPCA.
- Surprise your mother-in-law with flowers.
- Call to say if you are going to be more than ten minutes late for an appointment.
- Phone your hosts or send a thankyou-card if you were invited to dinner.
- Phone your parents and thank them for everything they have sacrificed for you.
- Do not feel sorry for the people who are cold in the winter – buy a few blankets and hand them out.
- Write the birthdays of family members, colleagues and friends on a calender and hang it next to your bathroom mirror, so that you won't forget them.
- Do not blame others if you have made a mistake – be willing to take the blame and accept responsibility.
- Take the trouble to memorise the names of people you meet.
- Concentrate not to say negative things about other people.
- Organise a bring-and-braai and invite the people in your neighbourhood.

Be a comforter

We all need to be comforted sometimes. In bad times we need someone to feel with us, who, like Job's friend, is willing to sit with us – even without saying a word. We experience God's comfort in our lives through the sympathy of people who offer us their consolation.

But not all of us know that the best way of being comforted in a time of hurt is by comforting others. You will always benefit from being a comforter. The Bible teaches us that brokenhearted people should be happy, because their suffering qualifies them for God's comfort.

Suffering makes better comforters of us. If you are suffering at the moment, look around to see if there aren't others who may need you. Make the time to offer them your comfort and sympathy. Make the time to support and help them. Then you too will experience the highest comfort.

 *Be a comforter*

When trees and plants feel the sun in the morning, they begin to live. The love that Jesus teaches about, isn't directed at the whole of mankind or at people we are not involved with. He talks about concrete love, about our relationship with our neighbour, about our behaviour towards everyone who needs us. (Hans Küng)

No man can live without comfort! Comfort does not consist of a flood of words. Comfort is a mild ointment on deep wounds. Comfort is an unexpected oasis in a great desert that restores your faith in life. Comfort is a soft hand on your forehead that calms you. Comfort is someone close to you who understands your tears, who listens to your tormented heart, who stays with you in your fear and uncertainties and shows you the stars. (Phil Bosmans)

Comfort can only be given through compassion in the true sense of the word: only a person who has been in similar circumstances can understand the suffering people experience. The best comfort is a person's presence and his silence. (F. Haverschmidt)

The true strong character flourishes in grief, his roots find a new mystical power in sorrow that transforms him into a personality that offers comfort and support to others. (Gerhard Beukes)

Be a comforter

Make time to comfort others

- Buy a special card or flowers for someone who is going through a difficult time.
- Listen to your friend's "why-questions" without giving quick solutions.
- Go and sit by a friend who has lost a beloved.
- Do not evade talking about the deceased.
- Organise food for a family who has lost a loved one.
- Offer to answer the phone.
- Let people who are suffering talk about their pain without interrupting them.
- Do not dwell on your own miseries in the presence of someone who is suffering.
- Reach out to and pray for a suffering stranger of whom you have read in the newspaper.
- Phone someone in a crisis situation to say that you care and that you are praying for them.
- Offer a lift to the doctor or hospital to someone who can't drive.
- Be willing to struggle through a crisis together with people who need you.
- Share your faith with someone who is suffering by telling him

Be a comforter

how God has helped and carried you in the past.
- Give a hug to someone who is in a difficult situation to show that you care.
- Buy a book of consolation for someone who goes through a difficult time.
- Pray with someone who is facing a crisis.
- Share God's comfort with someone by writing a scripture verse on a card and putting it in his post box.

Love with rolled up sleeves

The greatest commandment that envelopes all the other commandments is that we should love God and each other with the same love that God has bestowed on us. The test for our love towards God lies in the love we have for each other. This love may never consist of our words alone – it has to be evident in our actions. It is only when love is revealed in our works that it has true meaning.

This selfless love clashes with our human nature. It is impossible to exercise such love if we do not have a personal relationship with God. We ourselves are unable to love selflessly without expecting anything in return, but God enables us to love this way through His Holy Spirit that dwells in us. Make time to illustrate God's love for you by doing loving things for each other.

Love heals people – those who receive it, but especially those who

Love with rolled up sleeves

give it unconditionally. (Karl Menninger)

The gospel of love is the gospel of foolishness. It is about a love that involves pain, a love that is etched on the cross. When a person enters this love, he submits his pride, prestige and power to take the last place and to be everyone's servant. (Phil Bosmans)

The lost opportunities which people will regret most, are the opportunities they had to love. (F.B. Meyers)

Only true love draws people to you! Otherwise you push them away. Where people become humane towards each other in the love they share, heaven grows upon earth. (Phil Bosmans)

Make time to love

- Be sure that your love is always present in your actions.
- Prepare a light meal for a sick neighbour.
- Put a flowerplant on your colleague's desk.
- Put money in someone else's parking meter whose time has expired.
- Help an elderly person to cross the street.
- Offer to wash and iron a hospital patient's clothes.
- Offer to buy your sick neighbour's groceries.
- Give the postman a glass of icy fruit juice on a warm summersday.

 *Love with rolled up sleeves*

- Take a batch of homemade biscuits to the Old Age Home in the town where you live.
- Invite the neighbour's children to swim in your swimmingpool.
- Remember that the people who need your love most, are usually the ones who do not earn it.
- Make an anonymous donation to your favourite welfare organisation.
- Invite the new residents in your neighbourhood to church.
- Buy a bread for the beggar without him having to ask for it.
- Introduce yourself to your new neighbours and take tea and sandwhiches for them.
- Organise a Christmas party at the Children's Home near you.
- Buy a basket full of groceries for a family who has financial difficulties.
- Brew a large pot of soup and take it to a night shelter.
- Send a card to the children in your neighbourhood when they write matric or when they are confirmed in church.
- Offer to give the children in your neigbourhood a lift to school.
- Babysit your working neighbour's sick toddler.
- Send your domestic worker to tidy up your sick neighbour's house – or do it yourself!
- Collect blankets and warm clothes in your neighbourhood and hand them out to the people who need them.

Love with rolled up sleeves

- Get involved with your church's charity work.
- Visit the people in hospital who do not receive many visitors.
- Offer your help to people whose house has been robbed.
- Do something good for someone who cannot repay you.